Writing
for
our lives

Writing for our lives

First published in Great Britain in 2022 by Step Beach Press, Brighton

Copyright © Turning Point 2022

The right of Turning Point to be identified as the author of the work has been asserted in accordance with the Copyright, Designs and Patents Act 1988.

A CIP catalogue record for this title is available from the British Library.

ISBN 978-1-908779-59-5

Picture credits: All illustrations are the author's, except where otherwise acknowledged.

Printed and bound in England by Mixam UK Ltd

Step Beach Press, 28 Osborne Villas, Hove, East Sussex BN3 2RE

www.stepbeachpress.co.uk

stepbeachpress@gmail.com

Contents

Foreword

As chief executive of **Turning Point**, I am immersed in a world where belief and hope is deep. We are driven by the people we support and celebrate the many talents of every individual. The School of Art, featured creatively in this book, has given people a place to express themselves and so have our poetry workshops and other creative forums. It therefore gives me great pleasure to see the production of this book. People using their writing to convey thoughts and ideas, in some cases stimulating recovery and being a vehicle to drive their future. For someone who enjoys words, I have appreciated the diversity and expressive nature of the poems and it is a great honour to know that Turning Point has been a part of all the individuals' lives.

My thanks go to all the contributors that have made this possible and to Louisa Adjoa Parker for her role in advising and supporting the project. In particular I thank Chris Parker, without whom this would not have been possible. As a former Turning Point Trustee, he was inspired when someone we supported attended a virtual board meeting and read their poetry. The genesis of this idea. On behalf of Turning Point, I'd like to dedicate this book to everyone who has at times needed support and say that there are many organisations such as ourselves that are there to support you.

Julie Bass, Chief Executive

Louisa Adjoa Parker is a writer and poet of English–Ghanaian heritage who lives in south west England. Her first poetry collections were published by Cinnamon Press, and her third, *How to wear a skin*, was published by Indigo Dreams. Her debut short story collection, *Stay with me*, was published in 2020 by Colenso Books. Her poetry pamphlet, *She can still sing*, was published by Flipped Eye in June 2021, and she has a coastal memoir forthcoming with Little Toller Books.

Louisa's poetry and prose has been widely published. She has been highly commended by the Forward Prize; twice shortlisted by the Bridport Prize; and her grief poem, *Kindness*, was commended by the National Poetry Competition 2019. She has performed her work in the south west and beyond and has run many writing workshops.

Louisa has written extensively about ethnically diverse history and rural racism, and as well as writing, works as an Equality, Diversity and Inclusion consultant. She is a sought-after speaker and trainer on rural racism, black history, and mental health.

> *I was delighted to be asked to read and judge the poems submitted for this book, and I enjoyed reading every entry. Poetry, like all art forms, can be incredibly powerful – the simple act of putting words onto a page, telling your story to others, being heard – can be life-changing, healing and empowering.*
>
> **Louisa Adjoa Parker**

Turning Point
School of Art

Turning Point School of Art aims to give people we support across England and our employees opportunities to explore, appreciate and make art to support their wellbeing.

Turning Point School of Art bridges the gap between cultural institutions' participatory programmes and new online access points to increase wellbeing through creativity, curated by Professor Sarah Perks.

Rachel Huyton

I am the Team Leader at Haven House in Nottingham. It is a mental health crisis house that offers a recovery focused approach to encourage our 'guests' to develop their own personal skills, to learn coping strategies that will in the long term improve their future and outlook. I have always been involved in the arts which led me to working within the health sector, as I strongly feel that arts and mental health go hand in hand. I aim to blend my own arts background in a complimentary way to offer new ways of communication and encourage a creative voice. Currently I am in my last year of training to become a psychotherapist, my focus being an integrative personal approach that will continue to develop my own arts and mental health skills.

One of the most important factors that has a real human impact, is to be heard. Listening is a genuine skill that is integral to a person's recovery process. This combined with a trusting and therapeutic bond will enable positive change.

Shielded Pedestrian

We used to go from A to Z, but now we are lucky to reach B.

Tiers have become tears of frustration and angst as communities
weave their way through rocky seas.

Forced separation has set new boundaries to climb.

Human resilience, a powerful tool but on reflection
big lessons are being shared.

Humans are complex machines, a ship of woven vessels,
steering into the unknown.

We navigate malachite fathoms in the hope that we will return.

These waves are stronger than us.

Faltering tides weave pulsating ripples of discontent across grains of sand.

Mapping journeys we once had and new ones we hope for.

Herd mentality has become the norm,
moving from space to space blinkered behind the mask that hides emotion.

As herds we now live in close proximity and patience is tested,
rifts uncovered.

Do we now need to address protopia,
gentle steps towards joint improvement across the globe.

Realistic mindful thought based on care in order to reach a unified calm.

If we are to see this as a test of strength, we need to have resolve.

Nature has had a chance to shine and lift her head.

Nature will win. She will not be tamed.

Rachel Huyton

'Herd' by Rachel Huyton

Dear Drugs

For so long now have I believed
That I needed you so much
Living my world around you
Allowing you to be my crutch

I've loved you more than family
I've loved you more than friends
I've loved you more than I loved myself
I've loved you to the end

To me our relationship meant so much
I thought you felt the same
But now I know you didn't
To you it was just a game.

I thought you were there
It was you and me
Now the fog has lifted
Again I can see clearly

I always thought you loved me
I always thought you cared
You made me firmly believe
That I'd always need you there

You didn't take away my pain
Just dulled it for a time
I've relied on you so heavily
But my problems were still mine

You only care about yourself
You only care about your goal
To destroy so many lives
Without a thought for anyone
Not children, husbands or wives

Why do you think that it's okay?
Where do you get off hey gear?
Well believe me when I shout it out
YOU'RE NO LONGER WELCOME HERE

I'll never stop loving you
I know because I've tried
All the oceans in the world
Couldn't hold the tears I've cried

But I've finally learned to live my life
Without you ruling me
No more time, tears or money
Am I going to waste on thee

How naïve I've been for thinking
If I needed you, you'd be there
I should have realised sooner
That you really didn't care

I'm worth much more than you can give
I'm strong enough to break free
Life is too short and too precious
You no longer have a hold on me

So finally, please leave me alone
I no longer need you to survive
I can get through life just perfectly
Without you by my side

Your strong and powerful hold on me
Has broken at long last
Farewell, so long and goodbye to you
I'm leaving you in my past.

Marie Richardson

Heroin

This drug is nothing but evil.
It turns you into someone you're not,
It can make you lie, steal and cheat
The very few people you've got.
I wish that I'd never tried it,
Never picked up that first bit of foil,
Then maybe I'd still be the person I was:
Trustworthy, loving and loyal.
But I now understand it's an illness,
It's the drug which is acting, not me,
It uses you like a glove puppet,
I just wish my family could see.
My mum's often asked me,
Why my children aren't enough?
I wish it was that simple
Then this wouldn't be so tough.
If there was a way to make it easy,
I would have done it many years ago,
If there was a way I could travel
back in time

Marie Richardson

'Life in lockdown' by Lisa Harston

Michelle Graham

I'm a peer mentor for Turning Point. I started drinking at 15, I'm now 50. I've been through every abuse you can name. I also have mental health issues, ie hearing voices and bi polar. I've been on my own throughout the years – I buried my head in drink; I've lived on the streets for three years. Four years ago I got help with Turning Point. I did a detox and have been sober now for four years. The after-care was the best – I started throwing my self into groups even though I hated being with people (I love it now). After detox I had to fill my time so I started writing poetry and painting. I've now done open mic nights for poets, art exhibitions for my art, and trained to be a peer mentor which is so rewarding. I feel I can give a lot to other people's journeys... anything is possible.

Steps To Recovery

The power of control in the hands of me,
all emotions coming to the surface,
no more poison to push them down to the toes,
having to learn how to deal with them.

Getting up in mornings with no drink in hand,
fighting off the demon poisons,
shaky but wise,
like a flow of water brushing past the rocks,
learning to live all over again.

The pain I caused mainly to myself,
unloving,
uncaring,
mixed up mind of confusion,
a life not worth living,
out of control disappointments.

Trying to escape the Abuse of every kind,
torment in my brain,
physical pain from being thrown around,
voices that haunt and control,
the uncontrolled thoughts of dying,
the numbness in the head,
the bottle with words of hate,

the harm to self constant.

The recovery journey,

uphill and strained but amazing,

like climbing the highest of mountains,

but left so child like,

learning the skills of life.

Stepping stones hoping not to fall in,

sink into old ways,

been a year,

a year of learning about me,

allowing myself to let people in,

who am I?

feeling like road runner running off the cliff.

Downside mental health spiralled,

voices over take,

but for once in my life I have friends that understand me and that side of me,

group is so important,

for them and for me.

It felt strange to begin with,

but as I travel this road I am starting to settle in,

although the panic inside is all, still, very real.

Floating on clouds of marsh mellow

the journey I'm taking of inspiration and creativity

is just the best feeling of all,

without that poison inside me.

Michelle Graham

Carlina Whitmore

My name is Carlina Whitmore. I am a 42-year-old woman with a great passion for life and all its experiences, however this hasn't always been the case. My early life was good overall, but I always struggled with change and the emotional roller-coaster that comes with having eight siblings; as you can imagine, our house was always busy and we were always competing for attention. During my early 20s I engaged in a very unhealthy relationship which led to me being the victim of domestic violence. I was torn between knowing this was wrong whilst also absorbing what I interpreted as love. I used recreational drugs and alcohol as an escape from the reality I was living which then led to me having a breakdown and being admitted to a mental health hospital. I began writing during my time on the ward solely as a way of releasing the thoughts from my mind. I found that by putting those thoughts and emotions on paper I was able to process them quicker and really enjoyed the creativity of words. I have since continued to write and have published reflective articles around working in mental health, whilst managing my own difficulties. Following the death of my older brother through suicide, I decided to try my hand at writing a poem expressing all the emotion felt at the time of his loss.

The Day You Left

IN MEMORY OF MY BROTHER SAM: 02.02.1977–08.07.2021

The day you left
The darkness arrived
Like a power cut
Instant
Sudden
Unexpected
For a moment the world stopped spinning
Time stood still
Screams and cries filled the room
Then moments of silence followed
The storm had begun
It took away the sun
On the day you left

The day you left
Was the crossroad between
Pain
Sorrow
Regret and relief
Torn between our sadness
And you're longing for peace
So many tears
Have been shed since that day
As light turns to dark
We all cry, think and pray
The storm eased a little
Yet still there is no sun
Since the day you left

The day you left
The memories arrived
Like bolts of lightning
And flashes of light
Roaring like thunder
In our heads at night
Your curly blonde hair
Riding bikes outside Nan's
The way you were so proud of your daughter and son
You in the kitchen
Making tea for Mum
Sam, Marley, Delroy
Three brothers
Bonded as one
Your sisters Nay, Coz and Jade
Oh, how we wish we could see you again
So many memories
Some happy
Some sad
Of you being a brother
Son
Uncle
And dad
Memories we shall cherish
Come wind or rain
From before the day you left

The day you left
You did not stop being
My eldest sibling
My very first friend
Please have no regrets
No turmoil
No shame

You've taught us all to love more
To value each second
Those that have passed
And yet to come
With us all you will remain
Through all seasons
For all days
Like a storm cloud
Thrashing out rain
Our hearts will beat for you
Long after the pain
Of the day you left

I have noticed the moon now
And the stars shining bright
The storm is still raging
But there is a twinkle of light
A glimmer of sunshine
That will eventually fill the sky
Like our hearts fill with love
As the days pass by
Do not worry about us
Do not carry any guilt
We just hope you can now rest
Without worries
Sadness
Burdens
And fears
A final end to the cloudy years
Now that you have left

Carlina Whitmore

'Safe passage' by Paula Lane

Lola Askarova

Hi, I am Lola. I am a marketer, writer, blogger and seeker. I always loved storytelling, be it poems, stories, tv/film or animation. I wrote, designed and illustrated my first poetry book when I was 11. I love the alchemy of writing, the process of finding right words to describe feelings, insight and weaving them into the rhythm of a poem. My all-time favourite poet is Vladimir Mayakovsky, and I love haiku, poems by Rumi, Roethke and Frank O'Hara. My favourite British writer is Jane Austen.

Crisis describes the deep low that many of us hit from time to time. Anxiety, dread, numbness, existential emptiness, it feels like you are touching the void, and it can suck you in or you can face it. Life is a wave. If these two poems show what contraction looks like, Alive and I don't want to forget are all about expansion, the healing journey, discovering yourself, your true nature and coming back home.

Faces

I've imagined you so well for so long...
When the Universe puts your face on
The craving's back and illusion is strong.
I forget. I run and I burn.

I forgot how hard heart
Stabbing memories hurt.
Emptiness thought it caught
Me. Surprise—meet my void.

What is the matter, anti-matter?
I am painting fractals on atoms.
A silent Buddha's scream.
Self-organising chaos.

Reminder—self-inject
The love that I project.
Light for you, love for me.
I want to be free.

Lola Askarova

Alive

I ran barefoot
On the frosty grass
In the dark, dark night
When the moon was a heart
My feet burnt
My soul was on fire
I yelled songs
Into the starry sky
I laughed and laughed
Alive. I was ALIVE
Ablaze with love
Aglow with light.
Run and jump
And shout with JOY
There's nothing else left to do
This side of the void
I vowed to myself
To not fall asleep
To remember tall trees
And water that's deep
Fire dragonflies float up
With our hearts
Illuminating the void
And its endless dark.

Lola Askarova

'The Tree' by David Cottrell

Crisis

_____

Some days I am dead
I am swept
Into the darkness
Of insatiable madness

Like kraken
Shadows dragging
Me down
And I drown

Chained
To the rising dark
Swallowed by black
Darkness attack

Magic spells
Don't help
I am a shell
Spiralling into hell

Black tornado swirling
Hurtling
Spreading up my veins
All in vain

Today
It's like I left
Victim of theft
Lost and stolen soul

Don't wipe my tears
Dear
Accept
Today I am dead.

Lola Askarova

I Don't Want To Forget

How to not forget this?
To not let the memories fade?
To keep the fire burning
And see the wolf's starry eyes in the night sky?
How to remember
That the void is just a hand away
And that this body can be left behind.
That time is solid
Or rather doesn't exist.
How to remember
The truth in all its glory?
A shamanic drum is singing,
A story of a dragonfly.
Or is this an angel
With four blue eyes?
The fire roars inside, awakened.
The divine force is alive.
The mushroom goes back to earth,

We go back to lives

That we now know

Aren't what they seem.

Putting an old mask

On a new truth.

What next? How do you live now?

I breathe into chakras

Of worthiness and love.

A bolt of lightning in my hand.

An acorn in my pocket.

Tears in my eyes.

Sand in my shoes.

Glowing, buzzing

With an omnipresent force of creation

That is love.

Lola Askarova

'A walk in the woods' by Jenny Seals

John Nelson

I came from a family of five brothers and four sisters, 10 in total. My mother and father worked extremely hard to put a roof over our heads and place food on the table. My father was a strict disciplinarian and I didn't have a loving, intimate relationship with him. While it was much better with my mother, we didn't get hugs and told we were loved. Yet despite all of that I instinctively knew I was loved, just that it wasn't given or shown in the way I needed it. I then rebelled, without knowing I was rebelling. Looking back, I think the lack of intimacy and outward demonstration of love fuelled my rebellion. I then started truanting from school, taking drugs and mixing with the wrong company. It wasn't long before I started getting into trouble with law enforcers and finding myself in the judiciary system. These I call my wasted years where I made so many wrong decisions. I knew I was good at rhyming over 20 years ago but never did anything with it or wrote anything down until maybe 12 years ago. I was best man at my brother's wedding: I was thinking what I could say at the wedding and what gift can I give them... I then thought about writing them a poem which would cover most of my speech and make a good gift as well. So, I wrote a poem, printed it off on marble paper and framed it. The speech went really well and the poem caused many guests to be teary eyed. I then discovered how therapeutic poetry was, not only for me, but for others. Since then, I have wrote many poems for former colleagues who were leaving their jobs, also for weddings and funerals. I write poems on religion, gangs, drugs and many other subjects.

To Choose Or Not To Choose

I had no choice on the date I would arrive into this world,
No choice whether I would be a boy or a girl.
I had no choice in what country I would be born.
Isn't it amazing how in my mother's womb, I was secretly formed.
I had no choice whether I would be white or black.
Yet many choose to discriminate based on that interesting fact.
I couldn't choose who my parents would be,
So couldn't be sure if they would genuinely love me.
It's possible for love to be owned but yet never shown.
I guess the million-dollar question is;
if love is not seen then how can it be truly known?
If love is hidden then it's surely forbidden,
Locked in a secret vault and secured by a lock and bolt.
Love can be there but the possessors are either not willing to give it
or don't know how to share.
So many people have responsibilities but don't have the ability to respond.
By abandoning their responsibilities to show love, they miss a glorious
opportunity to create a meaningful and lasting bond.
Let's put it this way, making choices is like planting seeds.

Sow the wrong ones and you will end up with useless weeds.

I have a choice on who my wife will be.

Well, that's not quite correct; she also has to choose me.

I had the opportunity to choose who will be my friends.

I'd say, choose wisely because once a choice has been made it is difficult to make amends.

There is a parable that should be treated as law.

The parable states, "show me your friends and I will show you who you really are".

Let's face it, bad company corrupts good character.

If you hang around with thieves, pretty soon you'll need a barrister.

Pardon my expressions but I have a valid excuse.

It's a choice to sample illicit substances, and to carry on that misuse.

It's easy to point a finger but fail to notice the thumb pointing back at you.

This is a form of justification; while in that mind-set a person won't know what to do.

Some people choose to just sit on the fence.

But that choice doesn't really make much sense.

That's like burying your head in the sand.

This is another form of surrendering without raising your hands.

Some sources suggest that the average person makes 35,000 choices or decisions per day

With that in mind, our choices should be made wisely,

as wrong choices can lead many to go astray.

John Nelson

Maysie Morrison

From being a teenager, I have suffered with bouts of bulimia nervosa. The first time it happened, I spent two weeks in a psychiatric hospital. In my early twenties, I also experienced a scary episode of schizophrenia alongside reoccurrences of bulimia nervosa. This led to a 7-month hospitalisation in a psychiatric hospital and a 12-month stay at Douglas House Mental Health Rehabilitation Centre. However, since leaving rehabilitation, I have been living independently. I did some peer mentoring which led to some paid peer support work and I completed an undergraduate degree. It has been quite a journey. Yet despite everything that has happened in my life so far, I can finally say that I am proud of where I am. I am also honoured to now be working in mental health, where I can use the lessons that I've learnt to support others and to give back to the services which helped me.

Blurring Boundaries

I watched them, engrossed in reports,
and imagined myself poised there,
the pungent coffee urging me on,
post-it's a guide for my duties

Then I left the rehab's comfort,
and raced like youths on rollerblades,
a 'to do' list at home was gripping,
and mental health support braked

Today I work at that rehab,
fans whirring in the muggy heat,
my name badge a sweetener,
like those I'm offered with my tea

I now sense that I knew little,
of the trials that plagued the other side,
a stinging infection of woes,
but our work numbs the pain

Maybe hurt is a constant blow,
that can wildly haunt us all,
puncturing thick but delicate skin -

yet this means we are not alone.

Maysie Morrison

Unreal Reflections

My flesh pulsed as I was bolted down
to a chair spiked with roughened gravel,
'life's fool and cursed' the air spat,
it's screeching gusts a muddled siren

I was bitten with scorching poison,
as pain rattled through my veins,
my burnt features thrashed onto a mirror –
I lurched and choked on the ground

My anger was the dirty culprit,
driving the beastly bulges in my limbs,
it scarred me with deep craters – bruises
from felicities' ghosts

Yet, as I confronted my reflection again,
the chains were shod like cracking mud,
now a pool of bleak, blackened tar,
seeping through the soil's depths

My self-respect was the cure,
embracing even hopeless atoms,
gliding towards my reflection, to reveal
a complex, accepted human.

Maysie Morrison

Amidst The Madness

A space in time emerges,
amidst gritty mug stains,
and stinging flesh in water,
my steaming soul escaping
through angular windows,
feelings collapsing like mud.

A space in time emerges,
amongst scrawled pages
piled high like Jenga blocks,
soon to harshly topple,
so that my eyes gather dust,
and seep wet, just pain.

A space in time emerges,
between the chaos that surrounds,
the angry buzz of the TV,
the chatter biting my ears,
the hoarse roar of the hedge trimmer.

A space in time emerges,
so instead I shape for myself
a burrow away from disturbed peace,
savoring the comforting air,
breathing on the golden walls,
like they're luscious, bold pages
and I read a neat sentence –

It says 'you must write' – and I will.

Maysie Morrison

'Perch' by Rachel Huyton

Pete Singleton

The Colourful Choices

This poem seemed to just drift into place for me and for inspiration I used my lived experience of alcohol addiction and the interflowing issues of mental health. It evolved quite quickly, combining the traffic light imagery of the different symbolic colours and a nautical theme mixed with potentially perilous liquids. I would say I'm currently at a red light (according to my poem) as far as the potential for a relapse goes and I have been for almost a year now. To keep it that way I must always heed my own advice and be wary of any amber warning signs!

I'm Working on My Recovery

The sentences in each stanza are quite long, because I had a lot to say about this chance encounter with my new neighbour. We actually chatted about a lot of different things but his innocent question about what I do for work stood out to me as being one I would like to have a different answer for in the not so distant future.

It's not that I'm ashamed of being unemployed, it's just that as my recovery progresses the higher up my agenda finding meaningful paid employment goes on my long list of SMART goals.

As part of my recovery I intend to become a peer mentor and through helping others I hope to be that one step closer to realising my goal of financial independence.

The Colourful Choices

Red light status means I'm teetotal and I've stopped
My coordinates are locked whenever the anchor is dropped
Abstinence is an ordnance survey map where I can find the real me
My armor is on and I'm as buoyant as I'll ever be

Amber light's glow is like a tantalising flare
Avoid the liquid collision or go overboard, do I dare?
Hold on to the lifejacket of sobriety or just let go and accept my loss?
Notions of oceans of happiness or misery; amber time to decide who's boss!

Green light means just go, do it, have a drink
By then it's probably too late for me, I've disembarked merrily on a course to
sink
I've set sail for oblivion or perhaps somewhere near
When I'm lost out to sea; a fugitive harboring something I should truly fear

Pete Singleton

I'm Working
On My Recovery

I finally met my new neighbour for the first time last night
We talked for a good while, underneath my outdoor light

It's been weird not knowing what he looks like, or even his name
He shared much the same sentiments; he was thinking the same

He told me of his occupation and then he asked me mine
It's a difficult one that, because it seems to be something by which to define

'I'm unemployed right now,' I said, and he said 'oh well, you'll find something
soon'
It's a disappointing answer to have to give,
but from that feeling I've become somewhat immune

I could have said, 'I'm working on my recovery',
but I had no need to tell him that
I'm doing quite well at it anyway;
it feels like I deserve a promotion from where I'm sat

Last night had me thinking of my recovery,
what it's worth and what I'm working towards
A healthier and more fulfilling life;
enjoying the benefits of abstinence and reaping the rewards

I'm working with what I've got left from all the chaos that came before
I'm keeping up the good fight and the more I win,
I just want more and more

Hopefully, the next time we acquaint
I can tell him I've got money in the coffers
My recovery comes first,
but with that comes more stability and hopefully some job offers

Pete Singleton

Anna Abdulai

Since I was a teenager I've had problems with my mental health. Unable to navigate around what I found to be an incredible but confusing world externally and internally, I self-harmed for a while, realising I longed for kinder and more gentle ways of surviving and thriving. I started to put my feelings and thoughts down on paper. Invariably this would be in the form of poems. I've written poems on and off since. They usually come (quite literally) out of the blue, and, once down on paper, I hardly rework or reword anything that was frantically scribbled down or written up.

My poems usually come after a period of struggling with the ongoing challenges I face with my mental health but, almost invariably, writing them and re-reading them brings me a sense of relief, release and resolution.

This is a collection of poems that were written between 1996 and 2019.

Drop

Drop a pebble in the water
Just a splash, and it's gone
But there are half a hundred ripples
Circling on and on
Spreading, expanding from the centre
Flowing out to sea
There is no way of telling
How great the impact could be.

Anna Abdulai

Hope

They say the best predictor of the future is the past
But each day can be better than the last

Make it your mission each day to simply be you,
Regardless of whether your mood is yellow, green or blue.

Take joy in your achievements, however big or small,
Before you know it, you will be able to do more.

Don't give up, don't give in, or worry you can't cope;
There is always, always, always HOPE.

Anna Abdulai

Bright, Bright

Sunshine;
Don't hide away, don't disappear from sight,
Without your light, without you here
My daytime feels like night.
Waking to a fresh crisp morning
Opportunities are endless and real
Confusion from the darkness forgotten
In daylight wounds can heal.
A new dawn reveals the looming mountains
To be gently rolling hills,
The light from our brightest star
Serves to strengthen and resolve my will.
Hills, like dreams and possibilities
Stretch on forever and more.
Dreams, like childhood fun and games
Feel so innocent, so pure.
A sunbeam, when it's visible
Can take on different forms:
Sometimes playful, inspiring, uplifting
But when needed, it soothes and warms.
Prising open thick grey clouds
The sun comes beaming in
The strong bright light defeats the darkness
So happiness can win.

Anna Abdulai

'Haven' by Paula Lane

Helen Muncaster

I've been in recovery for 3 years from alcohol and cannabis addictions. I attended groups at Turning Point then went to detox. I'm now a peer mentor. I'm also a musician, I play guitar, sing and write my own songs.

Bin Man

You look like you've just crawled out of a bin.
You hide behind your beard and your heroin grin.
Your turning point is becoming a myth.
Can't let go of your heavenly abyss.
You won't venture out in case you start to feel.
Forever stuck in the past like a reel to reel.
Your body grows old, but your mind won't evolve.
Clinging to memories which will slowly dissolve.
Every few weeks you start to come round.
Step into reality where you should be bound.
But the fear creeps in, you crawl back within.
To your peaceful place, free from sin.
Take a risk or lose the chance.
Embrace this gift of life and dance, dance, dance!
Your oyster is waiting, you may find a pearl.
Your soul will guide you; life will unfurl.

Helen Muncaster

Vampire

I'll give you a search warrant
To rifle through my mind.
Be careful in dark corners.
Don't stand on a mine.
Avoid the empty wine bottles,
Pieces of broken glass.
Be careful: you might find
The corpses from my past.

The self-destruct demon
Who understands no reason,
Who controls all addiction.
The tantruming child trapped inside

The decay and the destruction
Disconnected synapses
Cobwebs embrace an aging face
Of a small child
Craving connections
I need my fix of affection
For this is my addiction.

You claw at my heart
With your nails till I bleed
Whisper in my ear.
Despair is what you feed on.
Your greed for destruction
Will know no bounds.
I surrender to you
As I drop to the ground.

The self-destruct demon
Understands no reason.
It applauds all addiction,
The tantruming child trapped inside.
I need an exorcism from this prison
Then wisdom and truth
Will rule my mind instead, this time

Helen Muncaster

Karmic Waters

I keep pushing through this endless tide
But there is no light in my eyes.
I keep on swimming through this endless mindscape
Only to be trapped inside.

I'm an architect of my own misfortune;
Even the tide lays the table twice a day.
Breath is just a clock ticking.
I have felt the feeling of my decay.

I've lost a friend; I've lost a lover.
You comforted me when I was down.
I've woken up from my coma.
The mist has cleared from my eyes.

I have burnt all my bridges
Cauterized my old ties.
And now nothing seems to stop me.
And I think I'm going mad.

I keep pushing through this endless tide
To karma karmic times.
And I'm ready to go out again
With light inside my eyes.

Helen Muncaster

'Departure 20.30' by Rob Padley www.robpadley.com

Jody Lee

Jody Lee, known as The Skinny Poet, has worked with recovery events for 15 years, writing pieces about his experience with addiction, abuse and recovery. He is now getting attention on the scene for his honest and unflinching poetry about the human condition.

Humans Being

For some people it is difficult
Simply to exist,
For some people getting through the day
Is like working a double shift.
Without a manager, without staff,
Without any support at all.
Some people feel all alone
As though they are standing
In a bustling mall.
Some people feel the need to scream
But cannot find their voice,
Some people choose to be strong each day
Although they never really had a choice.
Some people mask their feelings
With a smile on their lips,
Because some people taught them
A stiff upper lip is the only way to live.
Some people long to ask for help
But can't even hold your eye,
Some people put on a grown up show
While their child inside hides,
Frightened, confused and alone,
They've never known how to fill their space
Despite how much they've grown.
Some people cage their heart away
When they long to set it free.

Some people risk their heart each day
And pin it to their sleeves.
Some people open up their hearts
And live their life to serve,
But others see them as easy marks
And they don't get what they deserve.
Because some people think
That greed is needed
To get themselves ahead,
They carve a path through kinder hearts
Not caring where they tread.
Some people count their blessings
While dressing in the dirt,
Some people medicate their minds
When stressing makes it hurt to think,
Hurt to talk and hurt to be.
We can rant and shout and scream
But we only need to breathe.
Some try their best in every test
Yet still feel lost at sea.
Some people get called a mess
Because that's all other people see.
But in truth all of these people,
They're just like you, or me.
Some people, it amounts to us.
Good or bad, we're just humans...
Being.

Jody Lee

Water's Fine

Here comes that question:
Would you like a drink mate?
The sight, the smell, the sound, the taste,
This whole scene makes me...
Salivate.
It's as familiar as my ABCs
But I must refuse and choose
Whether I explain why.
Explain that if I take that ride,
If I awake that beast inside,
That it could destroy my life.
It could ignite every version
Of the person that I am,
And leave in its passage
Just the ashes of a man.
So do I, tell him? I mean...
I should be proud of my recovery, right?
Proud of my strength,
Proud of my fight,
Proud of my perseverance
To recover every part of me,
To discover my true self
From beneath the murky sea.
So I do. I say...
'No thanks, I'm in recovery.'
And he looks at me like I just landed
From another planet.

As though I'm not a man, but a Martian

An exposed fluctuation

In the time space continuum,

A tear in the fabric of his reality,

A complete irregularity.

And now I see he is confused;

To refuse a drink does not make sense to him.

'It's only one drink,

How harmful could it be?'

I've no time to explain what one drink is to me,

That one drink is just a tease,

The start, the first step onto a path

Which leads into chaos, darkness,

Into a maelstrom that barters for my very sense of self.

Nor do I have time to say

That it's one drink today

(Which is never one anyway)

And tomorrow it wouldn't change.

I would say, 'Well I've already had some

And it wasn't too bad, right?

I remember the night

I didn't fight

I got home in good time, So hey,

It's ok to drink today.

And then there's the fact

That I will feel so much better,

My whistle always sounds so much better,

When it's wetter.'

And so I would,

Then this pattern would unfold tenfold,

It would take hold of my rationale
And tear it apart like a wet paper towel.
Then my drunk mind
Once consigned to the liquor
Would not feel satisfied,
Would not settle until I added to this high,
Until I was flying like a shuttle,
Shooting off, full throttle, to heights unknown.
And I don't want to say
Even that would grow,
Would take hold, grow bold,
That I would unfold and no longer remain,
Feel no love, no fear, no pain,
Nothing but an unquenchable appetite
For my own destruction.
An infliction, a malfunction,
That rules my base functions
And overrides my will to survive.
That I could be lost for weeks, for years,
Caught in a complex catacomb of tears,
Tearing apart every routine part of life
Just to pursue an unattainable high.
I am an addict.
A tragic captive to harmful habits,
I'm one of the ten percent
who seeks blissful distraction
Through exterior transactions.
I fall slave to my consumption
If it is not kept in check.
Any time any stressors

Fire my neurotransmitters

And cortisol courses through my mind,

I want to find the opposing side,

To ride a tide of dopamine

In ways seen as obscene,

To flood my mind with a serotonin sea

And stray from civilised behaviour.

I seek out my demons and turn them to saviours,

Then worship them with fervour,

I serve them till my light is dim,

Until my frame is frail and thin,

Until my life is torn down from within,

Until there's nothing left but them.

And I don't want that,

They've already had so much.

I don't want to feel their touch,

Don't want my light to fade,

My true self to cascade like a flimsy house of cards.

No, I want to shine hard, like a star.

To drown out my shadows with me.

To be my absolute pure self,

I may not be perfect, but I don't belong in hell.

See, I just want to live my life,

To live in truth, with love and light.

To take each day at a time.

But I don't have the time to explain,

So I say ...

Thanks mate, =water's fine.

Jody Lee

'Queen' by Jenny Seals

Eternal Entomology

I'll give you a search warrant
To rifle through my mind.
Be careful in dark corners.
Don't stand on a mine.
Avoid the empty wine bottles,
Pieces of broken glass.
Be careful: you might find
The corpses from my past.

The self-destruct demon
Who understands no reason,
Who controls all addiction.
The tantruming child trapped inside

The decay and the destruction
Disconnected synapses
Cobwebs embrace an aging face
Of a small child
Craving connections
I need my fix of affection
For this is my addiction.

You claw at my heart
With your nails till I bleed
Whisper in my ear.
Despair is what you feed on.
Your greed for destruction
Will know no bounds.
I surrender to you
As I drop to the ground.

The self-destruct demon
Understands no reason.
It applauds all addiction,
The tantruming child trapped inside.
I need an exorcism from this prison
Then wisdom and truth
Will rule my mind instead, this time

Jody Lee

The Road to Hope

I put my first foot on the road,
Do I dare to hope?
This road is long and curved and slow,
It's nothing like the road I know.
The road I know has cracks and holes
And traps that swallow people whole,
It's overgrown and dark and cold,
Devoid of any hope.
This new road before me shines,
No cracks or traps or tangled vines,
Just signs that glow with warmth and light
Saying: this way to find hope.
My hope lay broke in chaos' course,
I'd paused my dreams and closed all doors.
I'd crawled from love and curled in corners,
Bound up in a rope.
Now the road looks clean and clear;
Though hunger lurks and shadows leer,
The shame they creep on,

Pain they feast on,

Fear and suffering they leech from,

All this dwindles as I keep on

Down this road of hope.

Now every step reveals more light,

Makes hopelessness seem less to fight,

With tests of courage, tests of pride,

I carry on in hope.

Now here I stand with open hands,

Where hope once slipped my palms like sand,

I cemented a sure-footed land

To build on with real hope.

Each junction walked's connection formed,

Each corner turned; a turning point.

Each new step takes my journey forward

Furthermore to hope.

I put my next foot on the road,

It may be long and curved and slow,

But step by step my strength will grow

And now I dare to hope.

Jody Lee

The Dark and Lonely Horse

The dark horse came and I jumped on,
He took me for a ride.
He promised me I'd be alright,
But now I know he lied.
He rode and rode and rode and rode
And I just held on tight.
I felt strange comfort in his stroll
So I didn't even fight.
I fell off once or twice you know,
But soon jumped straight back on.
This horse, he had become my friend
And how could I be wrong.
But soon the reigns no longer worked
And I quickly lost control.
The horse snickered knowingly
As it became more than a stroll.
I pulled the reigns to make him stop,
But he just carried on,
This comfy ride I'd come to know
Soon felt very wrong.
I rode that horse for years and years,
Not knowing where I'd been.
But you may know this rotten beast,
Its name ... was Heroin.

Jody Lee

'Happy Feet' by Rob Padley www.robpadley.com

Angela Peterson

I was a popular and outgoing person and then I married a narcissistic man who subjected me to complete solitude by convincing me that everyone but him was looking out for me, he beat me mentally, emotionally, verbally and physically on a daily basis for 19 years, I drank to numb the pain of the beatings, big jump beacause there is a book of crap I could write, Dual Diagnosis and Access Community Trust have played a major part too, I am now a recognised Peer Mentor and have won an award. I am proud of my current achievements.

Meditation

Sit on a chair and get relaxed
By breathing deep and slow
Then close your eyes and concentrate
on where you want to go.
Perhaps to somewhere calm and peaceful,
Where you will be safe and warm
To a sunny field or forest,
Where you can gather up your thoughts.

Look around and take it in:
The trees and blooming flowers
The birds singing in the trees,
The lush green grass, the clear blue sky,
The gentle breeze that's blowing by.

And you'll gently drift into another time and place
And your mind, that at first was rushing
Will have given up the race.
You'll find a log to sit on,
And then you'll glance above,
Thoughts of work and home
Will drift away, making room for love.

A love of being free
A love of feeling joy
A love of being at peace,
Of discovering your new toy.

That toy is meditation
To play with as you choose
For when you think the world is winning
and you really don't want to lose.

Just close your eyes and drift away
Into this wonderland,
Then life, you'll start to notice,
Does not have the upper hand.

And when it feels as though you're winning,
Get up and off the log,
Go back through the field or forest,
And come back to the world again.

The world of true reality,
That you must live in every day,
And you'll cope with any problem
That decides to come your way.
Because you have your secret place
Which you can visit any day,
You don't have to pay to go there
Just sit and think of what you saw today.

So now you know the secret
Make a small place in your day
For sitting and slowly drifting,
First there then back again.

If you see me, say hello and wave
And I'll return the gesture
But be happy meditating,
For your own peace and surety of mind.

I must go now but don't forget
I may meet you over there,
Maybe just for a minute,
But still, the thought is there.

Angie Peterson

Tara Auty

I am a 27-year-old who struggles with emotionally unstable personality disorder. As an aspiring mental health nurse who aims to work for CAMHS, I turned to writing as a way to share my mental health journey by documenting the highs and lows I experience on my blog, showing that recovery is possible. I was a guest at Beacon Lodge after an inpatient stay on an acute psychiatric ward. I used my time effectively at the service and feel I made a positive impact on staff and peers.

Hope

_____

Full of hope
Full of care,
A place to recover
A place to repair.

When I cried
You were there,
On my bad days
You were prepared.

I came here broken,
I came here scared,
Through all the fear
And all the tears,
Beacon Lodge was there.

Thank you so much
For all of your care,
You've helped me feel hopeful:
A future's out there.

Tara Auty

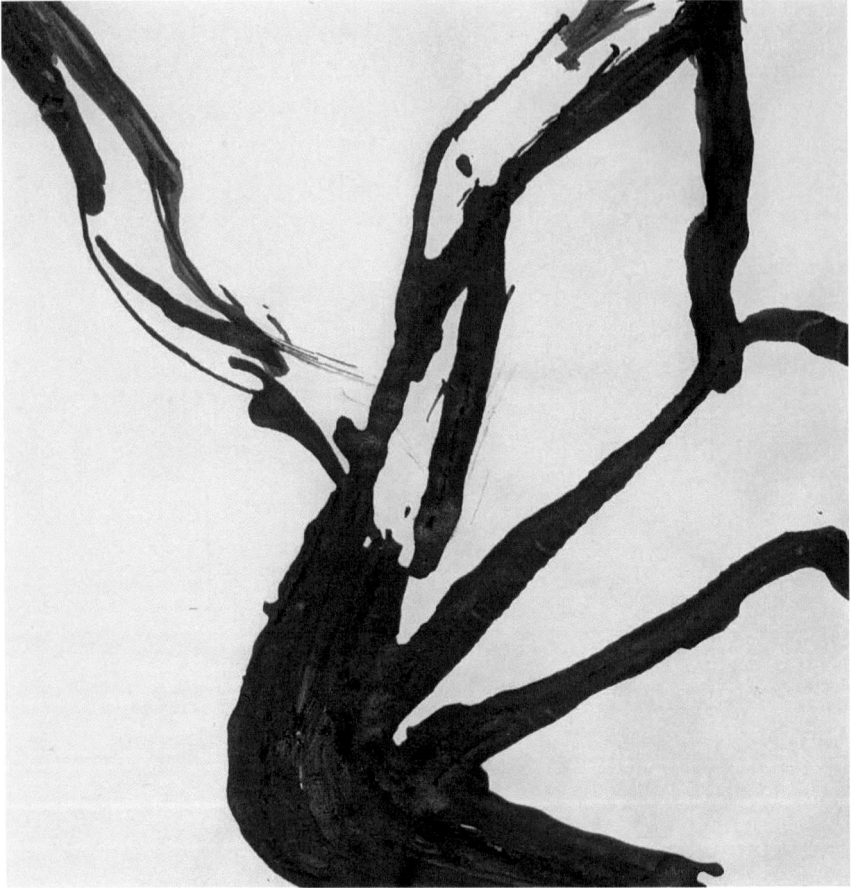

'Twigasauras' by Elizabeth Beaumont